This document is geared towards providing exact and reliable information in regards to the topic and issue covered. The publication is sold with the idea that the publisher is not required to render accounting, officially permitted, or otherwise, qualified services. If advice is necessary, legal or professional, a practiced individual in the profession should be ordered.

From a Declaration of Principles which was accepted and approved equally by a Committee of the American Bar Association and a Committee of Publishers and Associations.

The information provided herein is stated to be truthful and consistent, in that any liability, in terms of inattention or otherwise, by any usage or abuse of any policies, processes, or directions contained within is the solitary and utter responsibility of the recipient reader. Under no circumstances will any legal responsibility or blame be held against the publisher for any reparation, damages, or monetary loss due to the information herein, either directly or indirectly.
Respective authors own all copyrights not held by the publisher.

The trademarks that are used are without any consent, and the publication of the trademark is without permission or backing by the trademark owner. All trademarks and brands within this book are for clarifying purposes only and are the owned by the owners themselves, not affiliated with this document.

TABLE OF CONTENTS

Introduction.. 6

The Ketogenic Diet... 7

The Premise Behind Keto... 7

What to Eat and What NOT to Eat... 8

What you can Eat All the Time.. 9

What NOT to Eat... 10

Essentials of a Keto Smoothie or Shake Recipe............................. 11

Tips and Tricks for Keto Smoothies.. 12

Nuts and Seeds Fat-Based Keto-Approved Smoothie & Shake Recipes.................. 13

Brazilian Nut Shake with Greens.. 13

Creamy & Nutty Macadamia Nut Green Shake............................. 14

Creamy and Milky Pecan Shake... 15

Almond-Kale Green Smoothie.. 16

Nutty Raspberry Shake.. 17

Minty-Green Smoothie... 18

Creamy Blueberry-Nut Smoothie.. 19

Just Plain Nutty Smoothie... 20

Hazelnut-Mocha Shake.. 21

Brazilian Mocha Shake... 22

Gritty Coffee Shake.. 23

Coco-Nutty Coffee Shake... 24

Chocolate-Coconut Shake...25

Gritty Green-Tea Smoothie...26

Strawberry-Green Tea Morning Smoothie.................................27

Fruity Morning Smoothie...28

Creamy Wake-Me-Up Smoothie..29

Perky Green-Coco Smoothie...30

Blackberry-Hazelnut Chocolate Smoothie.................................31

Raspberry-Choco Smoothie...32

Coconut-Milk Based Keto Smoothies and Shakes.......................33

Turmeric-Spiced Coconut Milk Shake.......................................33

Tropical Choco-Coconut Shake..34

Lemon-Coconut Shake..35

Minty-Vanilla Coco-Milkshake...36

Nutritious Raspberry-Coco Shake...37

Ginger-Spiced Coconut-Milk Shake...38

Strawberry Coconut Shake..39

Hazelnut and Coconut Shake..40

Cardamom-Cinnamon Spiced Coco-Latte.................................41

Coco-Loco Creamy Shake...42

Chai Tea Smoothie...43

Raspberry-Flavored Chai Smoothie..44

Blueberry-Flavored Chai Smoothie...45

Chocolate-Flavored Chai Smoothie..46

Vanilla-Flavored Chai Smoothie.. 47

Raspberry-Coffee Creamy Smoothie..48

Boysenberry and Greens Shake...49

Blueberry and Greens Smoothie.. 50

Avocado and Greens Smoothie.. 51

Minty-Coco and Greens Shake... 52

Yogurt-Based Keto-Approved Smoothie & Shake Recipes............................. 53

Baby Kale and Yogurt Smoothie... 53

Nutty Arugula Yogurt Smoothie... 54

Hazelnut-Lettuce Yogurt Shake... 55

Garden Greens & Yogurt Shake..56

Italian Greens and Yogurt Shake.. 57

Creamy Blueberry-Kale Shake.. 58

Strawberry-Spinach Shake..59

Lemon-Mint Creamy Green Smoothie.. 60

5-Lettuce Mix Green Shake.. 61

Basil and Pine Nuts Shake..62

Rosemary-Lemon Garden Greens Smoothie...63

Lemon-Cilantro Greens Shake... 64

Blackberry-Chocolate Shake.. 65

Strawberry-Coconut Shake.. 66

Coconut-Melon Yogurt Shake.. 67

Berry Nutty Shake.. 68

Berry Overload Shake..69

Berry-Choco Goodness Shake..70

Lemony-Avocado Cilantro Shake...71

Strawberry-Chocolate Yogurt Shake..72

Milk-Based Keto-Approved Smoothie & Shake Recipes...............73

Choco-Coco Milk Shake...73

Nutty Choco Milk Shake...74

Gritty Choco Milk Shake..75

Creamy Choco Shake..76

Raspberry-Choco Shake...77

Strawberry-Choco Shake..78

Almond Choco Shake..79

Gritty and Nutty Shake...80

Nutty Greens Shake..81

Raspberry and Greens Shake..82

Spiced Almond Shake...83

Cinnamon-Choco Coffee Milk Shake..84

Mocha Milk Shake..85

Coconut-Mocha Shake..86

Nutritiously Green Milk Shake..87

INTRODUCTION

Hey! Thanks for browsing through this eBook on the Ketogenic Diet. All information here was gathered by me and I have tried to explain it in the easiest possible way for people like you and me to enjoy weight loss. The information I have provided are presented in such a brief way that it's basically centered on the things you need to know to start the diet.

This eBook is especially useful for people on the go. You can easily just grab and dump the ingredients in your blender and create Shakes and Smoothies to last you a whole month. There's a whole lot of variety to pick from and I hope you will enjoy them as much as I did!

The Ketogenic Diet

Ketogenic diet, likewise referred to as Keto Diet or simply keto, is a type of diet that makes use of the mechanisms behind diabetes. If you know someone who has diabetes, often this disease goes unnoticed and the person undergoes massive weight loss. Often, people who have diabetes used to be plump and can be more than overweight but with the onset of the disease and if not properly manage they lose weight and the process behind this is ketosis.

So, what is the ketogenic diet essentially? Basically, the diet is all about eating none to little carbohydrates at all—as much as possible. Your diet would consist mostly of protein and fat. Some sources would say that as much as 70% of the diet should be fat. This is the basics of the keto diet.

The Premise Behind Keto

When you put your body in a keto diet, something happens to it. Keto is not just a fad, it is actually based on a proven and repeatable scientific process.

Fact is, the body runs on carbohydrates. If you look at the food pyramid, it's the starchy foods which are carb-laden makes up the bottom of the pyramid. This means that the usual diet should consist more of starchy and grainy food groups. Now, if you eat too much of carbs, the body stores these excess foods as fats. What happens is that, instead of losing weight you are gaining more fats.

So, what if we remove carbs from our diet? What's going to happen? We did say that the body runs on carbs for energy. If we remove carbs, does this necessarily mean the body can't function because it doesn't have energy? NOPE! As a matter of fact, the body has a plan B for sourcing energy.

When the body runs out of carbohydrates to use as energy, it can use our stored fats for energy. What this means? Reduction of our fatty tissues! Leading to ultimate weight loss. What happens is that, our fats are utilized for energy which creates ketone bodies as byproducts—hence the term, ketosis. The state of ketosis is when your body is no longer burning up carbs for energy but fats.

WHAT TO EAT AND WHAT NOT TO EAT

As mentioned earlier, keto diet is primarily 70% fat, 25% protein, and 5% carb consumption. And logic will tell you that any food high in carbohydrates MUST be avoided 100% of the time. Therefore, you now know that in the ketogenic diet, not all food is available to you for consumption.

Essentially, your daily consumption of carbs is restricted to 30-50 Net grams per day, but others would advise you not to exceed 20g of carbs in a day. This is because all foods have a little bit of carbs in them. But let's say for your gender, height, weight, age, and type of lifestyle you need 2,100 calories a day. That would mean no more than 105 calories or 26.25-grams of carbs a day.
So, you need to be diligent in picking the foods you eat so that you will stay in a state of ketosis to lose all those belly fat, love handles, muffin top, arm flabs, and all those nook and crannies where fats just love to build-up.

So, to make things easier, here is a comprehensive, easy to understand and easy to remember of foods you can enjoy.

WHAT YOU CAN EAT ALL THE TIME

- **Nuts and Seeds** – please note that peanuts are legumes and does not occupy the nuts and seeds category. Peanuts and legumes are absolute no-nos in the keto diet. Generally, most seeds are widely accepted in keto.
    - Higher carb nuts: cashews and pistachios. Limit consumption. Two handfuls of these nuts are nearly equal to your one-day allowance of carbs.
    - Fatty, moderate carb nuts: pine nuts, hazelnuts, almonds, and walnuts. Use moderately for flavor and texture.
    - Fatty, low carb nuts: pecans, brazil nuts, and macadamia nuts. Can be enjoyed frequently to augment fat consumption.

- **Dairy Products** – Keep your dairy consumption to a moderate level and choose those that have lower carbs.
    - Lesser carb dairy (less than 3g of carbs per serving): Mayonnaise, brie, sour cream, and heavy whipping cream
    - Higher carb dairy (more than 3g of carbs per serving): cream cheese, half and half, Greek yogurt, cottage cheese, parmesan cheese, aged cheddar, and mascarpone.

- **Fruit and Vegetables** – Only green and leafy vegetables are 100% approved. But, you can enjoy some other vegetables and fruits in a less frequent basis because of their higher carb content.
    - Green leafy veggies: anything that grows above ground and resembles kale or spinach is perfect for consumption any time and every time.

- Moderate consumption of: lime, lemon, raspberries, blackberries, blueberries, tomatoes, peppers, eggplants, strawberries, coconut meat, starfruit, avocado, honeydew melon, cantaloupe, and others.

- **Protein** – all meat and poultry are approved but, we won't be going into detail here as we won't be using protein in our smoothies nor shakes!

- **Fats and Oils** – Essentially you are to stay away from processed fats like trans fats (margarine) and processed polyunsaturated fats (like heart-healthy margarine spreads).   Here's a list of what you can enjoy:
  - Lard
  - Coconut oil
  - Ghee
  - Butter
  - Macadamia nut oils
  - Avocado oils
  - Olive oil
  - MCT oil or Medium-Chain Triglycerides

- **Other foods you can enjoy**: Dark Chocolate, Cocoa Powder, and Spices. You can use sweeteners like monk fruit, erythritol, and stevia.

WHAT NOT TO EAT

Essentially, these foods are not allowed in the keto diet because of their very high-carb content.
- Legumes: peanuts, chickpeas, black beans, fava beans, etc.
- Tubers: such as yams, potatoes, carrots, and the likes.

- Fruits: oranges, bananas, apples, etc.
- Sugar: maple syrup, agave, honey, etc.
- Grains – cereal, rice, corn, wheat

Essentials of a Keto Smoothie or Shake Recipe

When making a smoothie there's basically four components that you need:
First, is to meet your keto needs which should be 70% fat. So, based on the list of food above you have choices between nuts, seeds, dairy, oils, low-carb protein powders, and even the avocado fruit.

Two, you need flavor in your smoothie or shake. That's basically choosing nutty-flavored shakes and adding spices to make it more flavorful. If you don't want to sweat it, you can always turn to chocolate powder for some outright deliciousness. And when used in right amounts, you can also enjoy berry-flavored smoothies and shakes.

Three, is your medium or liquid. If you want a very creamy smoothie then I suggest using avocado, heavy cream, yogurt, cottage cheese or even chia seeds soaked in water. And if you want something a little bit watered down, then make use of good old cold water, almond milk, or plain milk.

And last but not the least, the vegetables. I love to add vegetables to my smoothie to increase its nutrition and fiber. I always add a handful of dark green leafy vegetables to my smoothie, which you can always delete if you are not sold.

TIPS AND TRICKS FOR KETO SMOOTHIES

- If you want your smoothies and shakes to be cold, I suggest using ice cubes instead of water. I also freeze my berries so that when I make them in my smoothie they serve as my ice cubes. This also goes for other fruits like cantaloupe, avocados, and melons.

- Thickening your smoothies can be tricky. So, if you love thick smoothies, like I do, I hold off on the liquid until the very end. So, what I do is, I combine all of my ingredients in a blender except for the liquid (be it milk or water). I puree all ingredients until smooth and if it is hard to puree because there is not much liquid, that's when I slowly add the liquid until I can puree all ingredients until smooth and creamy!

- When using oil in smoothies, make use of oils than do not harden in cold temperature—such as olive oils, avocado oil, and MCTs. Lard and coconut oil would definitely harden and might be hard to mix in with your shake or smoothie.

- If the nuts and seeds do not ground as fine as you want it to be, you can soak it in the liquid mentioned in the recipe overnight before using.

- When using chia seeds, it is best to soak in the liquid suggested in the recipe for at least 10 minutes before pureeing.

- 1 cup of water is equal to 8 ice cubes. If you want to use ice cubes instead of water in your smoothies, this is the conversion to use.

Nuts and Seeds Fat-Based Keto-Approved Smoothie & Shake Recipes

Brazilian Nut Shake with Greens

Serves: 1

Ingredients:
- oz Brazil nuts
- 1 tsp sunflower seeds
- 1 cup water
- 1 tbsp MCT oil
- 1 cup Spring mix salad blend
- 1 tsp stevia, optional

Instructions:
1. Add all ingredients in blender.
2. Blend until smooth and creamy.
3. Serve and enjoy.

Nutrition information:
Calories per serving: 350; Carbohydrates: 7.28g; Protein: 3.69g; Fat: 36.74g; Sugar: 1.88g; Sodium: 22mg; Fiber: 3.8g

CREAMY & NUTTY MACADAMIA NUT GREEN SHAKE

Serves: 1

Ingredients:
- oz Macadamia nuts
- 1 tbsp chia seeds
- ¼ cup heavy cream
- 2/3 cup water
- 1 cup spinach
- 1 packet Stevia, optional

Instructions:
1. Add all ingredients in blender.
2. Blend until smooth and creamy.
3. Serve and enjoy.

Nutrition information:

Calories per serving: 485; Carbohydrates: 13.6g; Protein: 6.67g; Fat: 48.02g; Sugar: 3.1g; Sodium: 50mg; Fiber: 8g

CREAMY AND MILKY PECAN SHAKE

Serves: 1

Ingredients:
- 2-oz Pecans
- ½ cup water
- 1 cup whole milk
- 1 cup arugula
- 1 packet Stevia, optional

Instructions:
1. Soak nuts overnight in water.
2. Add all ingredients in blender.
3. Blend until smooth and creamy.
4. Serve and enjoy.

Nutrition information:
Calories per serving: 546; Carbohydrates: 21.3g; Protein: 13.4g; Fat: 48.87g; Sugar: 15.0g; Sodium: 113mg; Fiber: 5.8g

ALMOND-KALE GREEN SMOOTHIE

Serves: 1

Ingredients:

- 2-oz almonds
- 2 cups water
- ¼ cup kale torn
- ½ cup packed spinach
- 1 packet Stevia, optional

Instructions:

1. Soak almonds in water overnight.
2. Do not discard water, add all in blender.
3. Add all ingredients in blender.
4. Blend until smooth and creamy.
5. Serve and enjoy.

Nutrition information:

Calories per serving: 334; Carbohydrates: 14.1g; Protein: 12.6g; Fat: 28.4g; Sugar: 2.6g; Sodium: 23mg; Fiber: 7.6g

Nutty Raspberry Shake

Serves: 1

Ingredients:
- 2-oz macadamia nuts
- 2 cups water
- ½ cup raspberries
- ½ cup spring mix salad blend

Instructions:
1. Add all ingredients in blender.
2. Blend until smooth and creamy.
3. Serve and enjoy.

Nutrition information:
Calories per serving: 444; Carbohydrates: 16.0g; Protein: 5.6g; Fat: 43.4g; Sugar: 5.6g; Sodium: 21mg; Fiber: 9.4g

MINTY-GREEN SMOOTHIE

Serves: 1

Ingredients:

- 2-oz Brazil nut
- 2 cups water
- 1 cup Spinach
- 1 stalk celery
- 2 mint leaves
- 1 packet Stevia

Instructions:

1. Add all ingredients in blender.
2. Blend until smooth and creamy.
3. Serve and enjoy.

Nutrition information:

Calories per serving: 417; Carbohydrates: 10.4g; Protein: 5.5g; Fat: 43.1g; Sugar: 2.9g; Sodium: 50mg; Fiber: 5.8g

CREAMY BLUEBERRY-NUT SMOOTHIE

Serves: 1

Ingredients:
- 2-oz Brazil Nuts
- ¼ cup Blueberries
- 1 cup Spring mix salad blend
- 2 cups water

Instructions:
1. Add all ingredients in blender.
2. Blend until smooth and creamy.
3. Serve and enjoy.

Nutrition information:
Calories per serving: 420; Carbohydrates: 14.3g; Protein: 6.3g; Fat: 41.0g; Sugar: 6.1g; Sodium: 34mg; Fiber: 7g

Just Plain Nutty Smoothie

Serves: 1

Ingredients:
- oz Macadamia Nuts
- oz Hazelnuts
- 1 tbsp chia seeds
- 2 cups water
- 1 packet Stevia, optional

Instructions:
1. Add all ingredients in blender.
2. Blend until smooth and creamy.
3. Serve and enjoy.

Nutrition information:

Calories per serving: 452; Carbohydrates: 15.7g; Protein: 8.5g; Fat: 43.2g; Sugar: 2.3g; Sodium: 13mg; Fiber: 10.5g

Hazelnut-Mocha Shake

Serves: 1

Ingredients:
- oz hazelnuts
- 2 cups brewed coffee, chilled
- 2 tbsp cocoa powder
- 1-2 packets Stevia, optional
- 1 tbsp MCT oil

Instructions:
1. Add all ingredients in blender.
2. Blend until smooth and creamy.
3. Serve and enjoy.

Nutrition information:

Calories per serving: 324; Carbohydrates: 12.0g; Protein: 6.8g; Fat: 32.4g; Sugar: 1.4g; Sodium: 12mg; Fiber: 6g

BRAZILIAN MOCHA SHAKE

Serves: 1

Ingredients:

- oz Brazil nuts
- 2 cups brewed coffee, chilled
- ¼ cup heavy cream
- 2 tbsps cocoa powder, unsweetened
- 1-2 packets Stevia, as needed

Instructions:

1. Add all ingredients in blender.
2. Blend until smooth and creamy.
3. Serve and enjoy.

Nutrition information:

Calories per serving: 352; Carbohydrates: 12.8g; Protein: 5.4g; Fat: 33.7g; Sugar: 2.1g; Sodium: 22mg; Fiber: 4.4g

GRITTY COFFEE SHAKE

Serves: 1

Ingredients:

- 2 cups strongly brewed coffee, chilled
- 1 tbsp chia seeds
- oz Macadamia nuts
- 1-2 packets Stevia
- 1 tbsp MCT oil

Instructions:

1. Add all ingredients in blender.
2. Blend until smooth and creamy.
3. Serve and enjoy.

Nutrition information:

Calories per serving: 395; Carbohydrates: 11.9g; Protein: 5.2g; Fat: 39.6g; Sugar: 1.3g; Sodium: 13mg; Fiber: 7.3g

Coco-Nutty Coffee Shake

Serves: 1

Ingredients:

- 2 tbsps coconut flakes, shredded and unsweetened
- 2-oz pecans
- 2 cups brewed coffee, chilled
- 1-2 packets Stevia, optional

Instructions:

1. Add all ingredients in blender.
2. Blend until smooth and creamy.
3. Serve and enjoy.

Nutrition information:

Calories per serving: 445; Carbohydrates: 12g; Protein: 6.1g; Fat: g; Sugar: 4.15g; Sodium: 40mg; Fiber: 6.5g

CHOCOLATE-COCONUT SHAKE

Serves: 1

Ingredients:

- 2 tbsps coconut flakes shredded and unsweetened
- oz pecans
- 2 cups water
- 2 tbsps chocolate powder, unsweetened
- 1-2 packets Stevia, optional
- 1 tbsp avocado oil

Instructions:

1. Add all ingredients in blender.
2. Blend until smooth and creamy.
3. Serve and enjoy.

Nutrition information:

Calories per serving: 408; Carbohydrates: 17.4g; Protein: 4.9g; Fat: 38.4g; Sugar: 5.0g; Sodium: 40mg; Fiber: 5.8g

GRITTY GREEN-TEA SMOOTHIE

Serves: 1

Ingredients:
- 0.5-oz hemp seeds
- 1 tsp chia seeds
- 2 tbsps pecan, chopped
- 2 cups boiling water
- 1 tea bag, green tea or flavor of choice
- 1-2 package Stevia
- 1 cup Spinach
- ¼ tsp fresh lemon juice
- 1 tbsp avocado oil

Instructions:
1. Place boiling water, hemp seeds, chia seeds, and tea bag in a bowl or large mug. Let tea seep until water is warm. Discard tea bag and chill bowl of water.
2. An hour or two later, add all ingredients in blender.
3. Blend until smooth and creamy.
4. Serve and enjoy.

Nutrition information:
Calories per serving: 299; Carbohydrates: 12.5g; Protein: 4.5g; Fat: 28.3g; Sugar: 0.7g; Sodium: 50mg; Fiber: 6.9g

Strawberry-Green Tea Morning Smoothie

Serves: 1

Ingredients:

- oz pecans
- 1 tbsp sunflower seeds
- 2 cups of boiling hot water
- 1 tea bag, green tea preferred
- 1 cup arugula
- 1 tbsp avocado oil
- ¼ cup strawberries, chopped

Instructions:

1. Place boiling water, hemp seeds, chia seeds, and tea bag in a bowl or large mug. Let tea seep until water is warm. Discard tea bag and chill bowl of water.
2. An hour or two later, add all ingredients in blender.
3. Blend until smooth and creamy.
4. Serve and enjoy.

Nutrition information:

Calories per serving: 394; Carbohydrates: 11.04g; Protein: 5.2g; Fat: 39.2g; Sugar: 3.8g; Sodium: 30mg; Fiber: 4.6g

Fruity Morning Smoothie

Serves: 1

Ingredients:
- 3 medium blackberries, whole
- 2 tbsps chopped pecans
- 1 tbsp hemp seeds
- 1 tbsp sunflower seeds
- 1 tbsp coconut flakes, unsweetened
- 2 cups water
- 1 cup Spring mix salad blend
- 1 tbsp avocado oil
- 1 packet Stevia, optional

Instructions:
1. Add all ingredients in blender.
2. Blend until smooth and creamy.
3. Serve and enjoy.

Nutrition information:
Calories per serving: 385; Carbohydrates: 16.8g; Protein: 6.9g; Fat: 34.8g; Sugar: 7.0g; Sodium: 43mg; Fiber: 8.3g

CREAMY WAKE-ME-UP SMOOTHIE

Serves: 1

Ingredients:

- 2 cups brewed coffee
- ½ avocado fruit
- 1 tsp chia seeds
- 1 tbsp pumpkin seeds
- 1 tbsp sunflower seeds
- 1-2 packets Stevia, optional
- 1 cup Baby Kale salad mix
- 1 tbsp avocado oil

Instructions:

1. Place hot brewed coffee, chia seeds, pumpkin seeds, and sunflower seeds in a bowl or large mug. Let seeds soak in liquid cooled to room temperature. Then chill in fridge.
2. An hour or two later, add all ingredients in blender.
3. Blend until smooth and creamy.
4. Serve and enjoy.

Nutrition information:

Calories per serving: 417; Carbohydrates: 16.6g; Protein: 8.3g; Fat: 38.9g; Sugar: 1.4g; Sodium: 25mg; Fiber: 10.2g

PERKY GREEN-COCO SMOOTHIE

Serves: 1

Ingredients:

- oz Pecans
- 2 cups boiling water
- 1 green tea bag
- 1 cup Spinach
- ½ avocado fruit
- 1 tbsp coconut flake, unsweetened

Instructions:

1. Place boiling water, pecans, and tea bag in a bowl or large mug. Let tea seep until water is cool temperature. Discard tea bag and chill bowl of water with pecans.
2. An hour or two later, add all ingredients in blender.
3. Blend until smooth and creamy.
4. Serve and enjoy.

Nutrition information:

Calories per serving: 393; Carbohydrates: 16.3g; Protein: 6.5g; Fat: 36.8g; Sugar: 3.9g; Sodium: 60mg; Fiber: 10.6g

BLACKBERRY-HAZELNUT CHOCOLATE SMOOTHIE

Serves: 1

Ingredients:

- 3 large Blackberries
- 2 tbsps chocolate powder, unsweetened
- 3 tbsps Hazelnut, chopped
- 2 cups cold water
- 1 tbsp heavy cream
- 1 tbsp MCT oil
- 1-2 packets Stevia, optional

Instructions:

1. Add all ingredients in blender.
2. Blend until smooth and creamy.
3. Serve and enjoy.

Nutrition information:

Calories per serving: 363; Carbohydrates: 17.2g; Protein: 6.7g; Fat: 34.1g; Sugar: 5.1g; Sodium: 18mg; Fiber: 9.9g

RASPBERRY-CHOCO SMOOTHIE

Serves: 1

Ingredients:

- ¼ cup raspberries
- 2 tbsps chocolate powder, unsweetened
- 1-2 packets Stevia, optional
- 1 tbsp heavy cream
- ¼ cup Macadamia nuts, chopped
- 2 cups water

Instructions:

1. Add all ingredients in blender.
2. Blend until smooth and creamy.
3. Serve and enjoy.

Nutrition information:

Calories per serving: 333; Carbohydrates: 17.0g; Protein: 5.4g; Fat: 32.6g; Sugar: 3.5g; Sodium: 19mg; Fiber: 8.9g

Coconut-Milk Based Keto Smoothies and Shakes

Turmeric-Spiced Coconut Milk Shake

Serves: 1

Ingredients:
- ½ tsp Turmeric Powder
- ¼ tsp ginger powder
- ¼ tsp cinnamon powder
- 2 tbsps flaxseed, ground
- 1 cup water
- 1 cup coconut milk

Instructions:
1. Add all ingredients in blender.
2. Blend until smooth and creamy.
3. Serve and enjoy.

Nutrition information:

Calories per serving: 518; Carbohydrates: 16.5g; Protein: 5.0g; Fat: 52.1g; Sugar: 0.15g; Sodium: 36mg; Fiber: 2.1g

TROPICAL CHOCO-COCONUT SHAKE

Serves: 1

Ingredients:
- ½ cup coconut milk
- 0.5-oz dark chocolate solid
- 1 tbsp coconut flakes, unsweetened
- 1 packet Stevia, optional
- 1 tbsp coconut oil
- 1 ½ cups water

Instructions:
1. In a microwave safe mug, melt dark chocolate for 10 to 20 seconds. Mix in coconut milk and mix well.
2. Add all ingredients in blender.
3. Blend until smooth and creamy.
4. Serve and enjoy.

Nutrition information:
Calories per serving: 449; Carbohydrates: 13.4g; Protein: 3.5g; Fat: 45.2g; Sugar: 5.3g; Sodium: 37mg; Fiber: 2.1g

LEMON-COCONUT SHAKE

Serves: 1

Ingredients:

- ½ cup coconut milk
- 1 tbsp lemon juice, fresh
- A pinch of lemon zest
- 2 mint leaves
- 1 tbsp coconut oil
- 2 tbsps coconut flakes, unsweetened
- 1 ½ cups water

Instructions:

1. Add all ingredients in blender except for lemon zest and 1 mint leaf.
2. Blend until smooth and creamy.
3. Sprinkle lemon zest. Add mint leaf and enjoy.

Nutrition information:

Calories per serving: 445; Carbohydrates: 13.2g; Protein: 3.1g; Fat: 45.2g; Sugar: 8.3g; Sodium: 56mg; Fiber: 3.7g

Minty-Vanilla Coco-Milkshake

Serves: 1

Ingredients:
- ½ cup coconut milk
- ¼ tsp real vanilla extract
- 1 tbsp coconut flakes, unsweetened
- 1 packet Stevia, optional
- 1 mint leaf
- 1 tsp chia seeds
- 1 ½ cups water

Instructions:
1. Add all ingredients in blender.
2. Blend until smooth and creamy.
3. Serve and enjoy.

Nutrition information:

Calories per serving: 327; Carbohydrates: 12.57g; Protein: 3.71g; Fat: 31.6g; Sugar: 6.1g; Sodium: 34mg; Fiber: 4.8g

NUTRITIOUS RASPBERRY-COCO SHAKE

Serves: 1

Ingredients:
- ½ cup coconut milk
- ¼ cup raspberries
- 1 cup 50/50 salad mix
- 1 packet Stevia, optional
- 1 ½ cups water
- 1 tbsp pepitas
- 1 tbsp coconut oil

Instructions:
1. Add all ingredients in blender.
2. Blend until smooth and creamy.
3. Serve and enjoy.

Nutrition information:
Calories per serving: 408; Carbohydrates: 10.71g; Protein: 5.7g; Fat: 41.7g; Sugar: 2.0g; Sodium: 39mg; Fiber: 3.6g

GINGER-SPICED COCONUT-MILK SHAKE

Serves: 1

Ingredients:
- 1 cup coconut milk
- ½ tsp ginger powder or more to taste
- 1 small stalk celery
- 1 cup Spring mix salad
- 1 tsp sesame seeds
- 1 cup water
- 1 packet Stevia, optional

Instructions:
1. Add all ingredients in blender.
2. Blend until smooth and creamy.
3. Serve and enjoy.

Nutrition information:
Calories per serving: 475; Carbohydrates: 10.1g; Protein: 6.1g; Fat: 50.0g; Sugar: 0.8g; Sodium: 67mg; Fiber: 1.7g

Strawberry Coconut Shake

Serves: 1

Ingredients:
- ½ cup coconut milk
- 1 ½ cups water
- ½ cup chopped strawberries
- 1 tbsp hemp seeds
- 1 tbsp coconut oil

Instructions:
1. Add all ingredients in blender.
2. Blend until smooth and creamy.
3. Serve and enjoy.

Nutrition information:
Calories per serving: 418; Carbohydrates: 11.3g; Protein: 4.7g; Fat: 42.5g; Sugar: 4.3g; Sodium: 23mg; Fiber: 2.4g

Hazelnut and Coconut Shake

Serves: 1

Ingredients:

- ½ cup coconut milk
- ¼ cup hazelnut, chopped
- 1 ½ cups water
- 1 packet Stevia, optional

Instructions:

1. Add all ingredients in blender.
2. Blend until smooth and creamy.
3. Serve and enjoy.

Nutrition information:

Calories per serving: 457; Carbohydrates: 12.5g; Protein: 7.05g; Fat: 46.1g; Sugar: 5.3g; Sodium: 25mg; Fiber: 5.4g

CARDAMOM-CINNAMON SPICED COCO-LATTE

Serves: 1

Ingredients:

- ½ cup coconut milk
- ¼ tsp cardamom powder
- ¼ tsp cinnamon
- ¼ tsp nutmeg
- 1 tbsp chocolate powder
- 1 ½ cups brewed coffee, chilled
- 1 tbsp coconut oil

Instructions:

1. Add all ingredients in blender.
2. Blend until smooth and creamy.
3. Serve and enjoy.

Nutrition information:

Calories per serving: 362; Carbohydrates: 7.5g; Protein: 3.8g; Fat: 38.7g; Sugar: 0.1g; Sodium: 23mg; Fiber: 2.2g

COCO-LOCO CREAMY SHAKE

Serves: 1

Ingredients:

- ½ cup coconut milk
- 2 tbsps Dutch-processed cocoa powder, unsweetened
- 1 cup brewed coffee, chilled
- 1-2 packets Stevia
- 1 tbsp hemp seeds

Instructions:

1. Add all ingredients in blender.
2. Blend until smooth and creamy.
3. Serve and enjoy.

Nutrition information:

Calories per serving: 354; Carbohydrates: 16.2g; Protein: 6.8g; Fat: 34.6g; Sugar: 4.4g; Sodium: 26mg; Fiber: 6.6g

CHAI TEA SMOOTHIE

Serves: 1

Ingredients:

- 1 cups boiling water
- 1 black tea bag
- ¼ tsp ginger
- ¼ tsp cinnamon
- ¼ tsp cardamom powder
- 2 packets Stevia or as desired
- 1 cup coconut milk

Instructions:

1. In a large mug, mix boiling water, ginger, cinnamon, and cardamom powder. Add tea bag and let it steep until liquid is cool. Remove tea bag and squeeze out excess liquid and discard. Refrigerate liquid with spices until chilled. You can even transfer it in an ice cube tray and freeze.
2. Later, add all ingredients in blender.
3. Blend until smooth and creamy.
4. Serve and enjoy.

Nutrition information:

Calories per serving: 453; Carbohydrates: 10.33g; Protein: 4.7g; Fat: 48.3g; Sugar: 0.03g; Sodium: 42mg; Fiber: 0.6g

Raspberry-Flavored Chai Smoothie

Serves: 1

Ingredients:
- 1 ¼ cups boiling water
- 1 black tea bag
- ¼ tsp ginger
- ¼ tsp cinnamon
- ¼ tsp cardamom powder
- 2 packets Stevia or as desired
- ¾ cup coconut milk
- ¼ cup raspberries

Instructions:
1. In a large mug, mix boiling water, ginger, cinnamon, and cardamom powder. Add tea bag and let it steep until liquid is cool. Remove tea bag and squeeze out excess liquid and discard. Refrigerate liquid with spices until chilled. You can even transfer it in an ice cube tray and freeze.
2. Add all ingredients in blender.
3. Blend until smooth and creamy.
4. Serve and enjoy.

Nutrition information:
Calories per serving: 357; Carbohydrates: 12.4g; Protein: 3.9g; Fat: 36.4g; Sugar: 1.4g; Sodium: 44mg; Fiber: 2.6g

BLUEBERRY-FLAVORED CHAI SMOOTHIE

Serves: 1

Ingredients:

- 1 ½ cups boiling water
- 1 black tea bag
- ¼ tsp ginger
- ¼ tsp cinnamon
- ¼ tsp cardamom powder
- 2 packets Stevia or as desired
- ½ cup coconut milk
- ½ cup blueberries
- 1 tbsp avocado oil

Instructions:

1. In a large mug, mix boiling water, ginger, cinnamon, and cardamom powder. Add tea bag and let it steep until liquid is cool. Remove tea bag and squeeze out excess liquid and discard. Refrigerate liquid with spices until chilled. You can even transfer it in an ice cube tray and freeze.
2. Add all ingredients in blender.
3. Blend until smooth and creamy.
4. Serve and enjoy.

Nutrition information:

Calories per serving: 396; Carbohydrates: 17.9g; Protein: 3.0g; Fat: 38.4g; Sugar: 7.4g; Sodium: 37mg; Fiber: 2.4g

CHOCOLATE-FLAVORED CHAI SMOOTHIE

Serves: 1

Ingredients:

- 1 ½ cups boiling water
- 1 black tea bag
- ¼ tsp ginger
- ¼ tsp cinnamon
- ¼ tsp cardamom powder
- 2 packets Stevia or as desired
- ½ cup coconut milk
- 2 tbsps Dutch processed cocoa powder, unsweetened
- 1 tbsp MCT oil

Instructions:

1. In a large mug, mix boiling water, ginger, cinnamon, and cardamom powder. Add tea bag and let it steep until liquid is cool. Remove tea bag and squeeze out excess liquid and discard. Refrigerate liquid with spices until chilled. You can even transfer it in an ice cube tray and freeze.
2. Add all ingredients in blender.
3. Blend until smooth and creamy.
4. Serve and enjoy.

Nutrition information:

Calories per serving: 374; Carbohydrates: 13.4g; Protein: 4.4g; Fat: 39.2g; Sugar: 0.2g; Sodium: 31mg; Fiber: 3.8g

Vanilla-Flavored Chai Smoothie

Serves: 1

Ingredients:

- 1 ½ cups boiling water
- 1 black tea bag
- ¼ tsp ginger
- ¼ tsp cinnamon
- ¼ tsp cardamom powder
- 2 packets Stevia or as desired
- ½ cup coconut milk
- 1 tsp real vanilla extract
- ¼ avocado fruit

Instructions:

1. In a large mug, mix boiling water, ginger, cinnamon, and cardamom powder. Add tea bag and let it steep until liquid is cool. Remove tea bag and squeeze out excess liquid and discard. Refrigerate liquid with spices until chilled. You can even transfer it in an ice cube tray and freeze.
2. Add all ingredients in blender.
3. Blend until smooth and creamy.
4. Serve and enjoy.

Nutrition information:

Calories per serving: 323; Carbohydrates: 12.0g; Protein: 3.4g; Fat: 31.5g; Sugar: 0.9g; Sodium: 33mg; Fiber: 4.0g

RASPBERRY-COFFEE CREAMY SMOOTHIE

Serves: 1

Ingredients:

- ½ cup coconut milk
- 1 ½ cups brewed coffee, chilled
- ¼ cup Raspberries
- ¼ avocado fruit
- 2 packets Stevia or more to taste
- 1 tsp chia seeds

Instructions:

1. Add all ingredients in blender.
2. Blend until smooth and creamy.
3. Serve and enjoy.

Nutrition information:

Calories per serving: 346; Carbohydrates: 15.2g; Protein: 4.9g; Fat: 33.2g; Sugar: 1.7g; Sodium: 26mg; Fiber: 7.0g

BOYSENBERRY AND GREENS SHAKE

Serves: 1

Ingredients:

- ½ cup coconut milk
- 1 ½ cups water
- ½ cup Boysenberry
- 2 packets Stevia, or as needed
- 1 cup Baby Kale salad mix
- 1 tbsp MCT oil

Instructions:

1. Add all ingredients in blender.
2. Blend until smooth and creamy.
3. Serve and enjoy.

Nutrition information:

Calories per serving: 381; Carbohydrates: 14.6g; Protein: 3.7g; Fat: 38.0g; Sugar: 4.9g; Sodium: 29mg; Fiber: 4.1g

BLUEBERRY AND GREENS SMOOTHIE

Serves: 1

Ingredients:
- ½ cup coconut milk
- 1 ½ cups water
- ½ cup blueberries
- 2 packets Stevia, or as needed
- 1 cup arugula
- 1 tbsp hemp seeds

Instructions:
1. Add all ingredients in blender.
2. Blend until smooth and creamy.
3. Serve and enjoy.

Nutrition information:
Calories per serving: 321; Carbohydrates: 18.4g; Protein: 5.2g; Fat: 29.0g; Sugar: 8.0g; Sodium: 29mg; Fiber: 2.9g

Avocado and Greens Smoothie

Serves: 1

Ingredients:
- ½ cup coconut milk
- 1 ½ cups water
- ½ Avocado fruit
- 2 packets Stevia, or as needed
- 1 cup Spring mix greens
- 1 tbsp avocado oil

Instructions:
1. Add all ingredients in blender.
2. Blend until smooth and creamy.
3. Serve and enjoy.

Nutrition information:
Calories per serving: 439; Carbohydrates: 16.1g; Protein: 6.5g; Fat: 43.4g; Sugar: 1.0g; Sodium: 37mg; Fiber: 7.7g

MINTY-COCO AND GREENS SHAKE

Serves: 1

Ingredients:

- ½ cup coconut milk
- 1 ½ cups water
- 2 peppermint leaves
- 2 packets Stevia, or as needed
- 1 cup 50/50 salad mix
- 1 tbsp coconut oil

Instructions:

1. Add all ingredients in blender.
2. Blend until smooth and creamy.
3. Serve and enjoy.

Nutrition information:

Calories per serving: 344; Carbohydrates: 5.8g; Protein: 2.7g; Fat: 37.8g; Sugar: 0.1g; Sodium: 29mg; Fiber: 0.3g

Yogurt-Based Keto-Approved Smoothie & Shake Recipes

Baby Kale and Yogurt Smoothie

Serves: 1

Ingredients:

- 1 cup whole milk yogurt
- 1 cup baby kale greens
- 1 packet Stevia, or more to taste
- 1 tbsp MCT oil
- 1 tbsp sunflower seeds
- 1 cup water

Instructions:

1. Add all ingredients in blender.
2. Blend until smooth and creamy.
3. Serve and enjoy.

Nutrition information:

Calories per serving: 329; Carbohydrates: 15.6g; Protein: 11.0g; Fat: 26.2g; Sugar: 12.0g; Sodium: 124mg; Fiber: 1.3g

Nutty Arugula Yogurt Smoothie

Serves: 1

Ingredients:

- 1 cup whole milk yogurt
- 1 cup baby arugula
- 1 packet Stevia, or more to taste
- 1 tbsp avocado oil
- 2 tbsps macadamia nuts
- 1 cup water

Instructions:

1. Add all ingredients in blender.
2. Blend until smooth and creamy.
3. Serve and enjoy.

Nutrition information:

Calories per serving: 399; Carbohydrates: 15.5g; Protein: 10.3g; Fat: 34.8g; Sugar: 12.6g; Sodium: 124mg; Fiber: 1.8g

HAZELNUT-LETTUCE YOGURT SHAKE

Serves: 1

Ingredients:

- 1 cup whole milk yogurt
- 1 cup lettuce chopped
- 1 packet Stevia, or more to taste
- 1 tbsp olive oil
- 3 tbsps Hazelnut chopped
- 1 cup water

Instructions:

1. Add all ingredients in blender.
2. Blend until smooth and creamy.
3. Serve and enjoy.

Nutrition information:

Calories per serving: 412; Carbohydrates: 17.2g; Protein: 12.5g; Fat: 34.7g; Sugar: 12.9g; Sodium: 120mg; Fiber: 2.7g

GARDEN GREENS & YOGURT SHAKE

Serves: 1

Ingredients:

- 1 cup whole milk yogurt
- 1 cup Garden greens
- 1 packet Stevia, or more to taste
- 1 tbsp MCT oil
- 1 tbsp flaxseed, ground
- 1 cup water

Instructions:

1. Add all ingredients in blender.
2. Blend until smooth and creamy.
3. Serve and enjoy.

Nutrition information:

Calories per serving: 334; Carbohydrates: 17.2g; Protein: 11.2g; Fat: 26.0g; Sugar: 12.1g; Sodium: 136mg; Fiber: 3.9g

ITALIAN GREENS AND YOGURT SHAKE

Serves: 1

Ingredients:
- 1 cup whole milk yogurt
- 1 cup Italian greens
- 1 packet Stevia, or more to taste
- 1 tbsp olive oil
- 1 tbsp hemp seeds
- 1 cup water

Instructions:
1. Add all ingredients in blender.
2. Blend until smooth and creamy.
3. Serve and enjoy.

Nutrition information:

Calories per serving: 333; Carbohydrates: 17.2g; Protein: 11.2g; Fat: 25.9g; Sugar: 12.1g; Sodium: 137mg; Fiber: 3.9g

CREAMY BLUEBERRY-KALE SHAKE

Serves: 1

Ingredients:

- ½ cup whole milk yogurt
- 1 cup baby kale greens
- 1 packet Stevia, or more to taste
- 1 tbsp MCT oil
- ¼ cup blueberries
- 1 tbsp pepitas
- 1 tbsp flaxseed, ground
- 1 ½ cups water

Instructions:

1. Add all ingredients in blender.
2. Blend until smooth and creamy.
3. Serve and enjoy.

Nutrition information:

Calories per serving: 307; Carbohydrates: 16.6g; Protein: 8.7g; Fat: 24.8g; Sugar: 10.0g; Sodium: 71mg; Fiber: 3.9g

STRAWBERRY-SPINACH SHAKE

Serves: 1

Ingredients:

- ½ cup whole milk yogurt
- 1 cup spinach
- 1 packet Stevia, or more to taste
- 1 tbsp MCT oil
- ½ cup strawberries, chopped
- 1 tbsp hemp seeds
- 1 tbsp flaxseed, ground
- 1 ½ cups water

Instructions:

1. Add all ingredients in blender.
2. Blend until smooth and creamy.
3. Serve and enjoy.

Nutrition information:

Calories per serving: 334; Carbohydrates: 18.9g; Protein: 9.4g; Fat: 26.7g; Sugar: 10.3g; Sodium: 90mg; Fiber: 5.9g

LEMON-MINT CREAMY GREEN SMOOTHIE

Serves: 1

Ingredients:

- ½ cup whole milk yogurt
- 1 cup Spring mix salad greens, packed
- 1 packet Stevia, or more to taste
- 1 tbsp MCT oil
- 1 tsp lemon juice, fresh
- 2 peppermint leaves
- 1 tbsp chia seeds
- 1 tbsp flaxseed, ground
- 1 ½ cups water

Instructions:

1. Add all ingredients in blender.
2. Blend until smooth and creamy.
3. Serve and enjoy.

Nutrition information:

Calories per serving: 326; Carbohydrates: 17.1g; Protein: 9.4g; Fat: 26.3g; Sugar: 6.1g; Sodium: 91mg; Fiber: 8.4g

5-Lettuce Mix Green Shake

Serves: 1

Ingredients:

- ¾ cup whole milk yogurt
- 2 cups 5-lettuce mix salad greens
- 1 packet Stevia, or more to taste
- 1 tbsp MCT oil
- 1 tbsp chia seeds
- 1 ½ cups water

Instructions:

1. Add all ingredients in blender.
2. Blend until smooth and creamy.
3. Serve and enjoy.

Nutrition information:

Calories per serving: 320; Carbohydrates: 19.1g; Protein: 10.4g; Fat: 24.2g; Sugar: 9.6g; Sodium: 126mg; Fiber: 7.1g

BASIL AND PINE NUTS SHAKE

Serves: 1

Ingredients:

- ½ cup whole milk yogurt
- 1 cup spring mix salad greens
- 1 packet Stevia, or more to taste
- 1 tbsp olive oil
- 2 tbsps pine nuts, chopped
- 2 tbsps walnuts, chopped
- 10 basil leaves
- 1 tbsp hemp seeds
- 1 ½ cups water

Instructions:

1. Add all ingredients in blender.
2. Blend until smooth and creamy.
3. Serve and enjoy.

Nutrition information:

Calories per serving: 465; Carbohydrates: 14.6g; Protein: 11.6g; Fat: 43.2g; Sugar: 7.4g; Sodium: 81mg; Fiber: 3.5g

ROSEMARY-LEMON GARDEN GREENS SMOOTHIE

Serves: 1

Ingredients:
- ½ cup whole milk yogurt
- 1 cup Garden greens
- 1 packet Stevia, or more to taste
- 1 tbsp olive oil
- 1 stalk fresh rosemary
- 1 tbsp lemon juice, fresh
- 1 tbsp pepitas
- 1 tbsp flaxseed, ground
- 1 ½ cups water

Instructions:
1. Add all ingredients in blender.
2. Blend until smooth and creamy.
3. Serve and enjoy.

Nutrition information:

Calories per serving: 312; Carbohydrates: 14.7g; Protein: 9.7g; Fat: 25.9g; Sugar: 8.6g; Sodium: 75mg; Fiber: 4g

LEMON-CILANTRO GREENS SHAKE

Serves: 1

Ingredients:

- ½ cup whole milk yogurt
- 1 cup baby kale greens
- 1 packet Stevia, or more to taste
- 1 tbsp avocado oil
- 1 tbsp lemon juice, fresh
- 1 tsp cilantro, chopped
- ¼ avocado fruit
- 1 tbsp flaxseed, ground
- 1 ½ cups water

Instructions:

1. Add all ingredients in blender.
2. Blend until smooth and creamy.
3. Serve and enjoy.

Nutrition information:

Calories per serving: 345; Carbohydrates: 16.4g; Protein: 7.9g; Fat: 29.9g; Sugar: 6.9g; Sodium: 76mg; Fiber: 6.8g

BLACKBERRY-CHOCOLATE SHAKE

Serves: 1

Ingredients:
- ½ cup whole milk yogurt
- ¼ cup blackberries
- 1 packet Stevia, or more to taste
- 1 tbsp MCT oil
- 1 tbsp Dutch-processed cocoa powder
- 2 tbsps Macadamia nuts, chopped
- 1 ½ cups water

Instructions:
1. Add all ingredients in blender.
2. Blend until smooth and creamy.
3. Serve and enjoy.

Nutrition information:
Calories per serving: 463; Carbohydrates: 17.9g; Protein: 8.5g; Fat: 43.9g; Sugar: 9.1g; Sodium: 67mg; Fiber: 6.8g

STRAWBERRY-COCONUT SHAKE

Serves: 1

Ingredients:
- ½ cup whole milk yogurt
- 1 packet Stevia, or more to taste
- 1 tbsp MCT oil
- ¼ cup strawberries, chopped
- 1 tbsp coconut flakes, unsweetened
- 1 tbsp hemp seeds
- 1 ½ cups water

Instructions:
1. Add all ingredients in blender.
2. Blend until smooth and creamy.
3. Serve and enjoy.

Nutrition information:

Calories per serving: 282; Carbohydrates: 14.0g; Protein: 6.5g; Fat: 23.7g; Sugar: 9.6g; Sodium: 80mg; Fiber: 2g

COCONUT-MELON YOGURT SHAKE

Serves: 1

Ingredients:

- ¼ cup whole milk yogurt
- 1 packet Stevia, or more to taste
- 1 tbsp coconut oil
- ½ cup melon, slices
- 1 tbsp coconut flakes, unsweetened
- 1 tbsp chia seeds
- 1 ½ cups water

Instructions:

1. Add all ingredients in blender.
2. Blend until smooth and creamy.
3. Serve and enjoy.

Nutrition information:

Calories per serving: 278; Carbohydrates: 19.8g; Protein: 5.4g; Fat: 21.6g; Sugar: 11.8g; Sodium: 67mg; Fiber: 6.2g

Berry Nutty Shake

Serves: 1

Ingredients:

- ½ cup whole milk yogurt
- 1 packet Stevia, or more to taste
- ¼ cup boysenberries
- ¼ cup Blackberry
- ¼ cup strawberries, chopped
- 1 tbsp hemp seeds
- 1 tbsp pepitas
- 1 tbsp chia seeds
- 1 ½ cups water

Instructions:

1. Add all ingredients in blender.
2. Blend until smooth and creamy.
3. Serve and enjoy.

Nutrition information:

Calories per serving: 283; Carbohydrates: 26.2g; Protein: 11.8g; Fat: 16.9g; Sugar: 12.1g; Sodium: 69mg; Fiber: 10.6g

BERRY OVERLOAD SHAKE

Serves: 1

Ingredients:

- ½ cup whole milk yogurt
- 1 packet Stevia, or more to taste
- ¼ cup blueberries
- ¼ cup boysenberries
- ¼ cup Blackberry
- ¼ cup strawberries, chopped
- 1 tbsp avocado oil
- 1 ½ cups water

Instructions:

1. Add all ingredients in blender.
2. Blend until smooth and creamy.
3. Serve and enjoy.

Nutrition information:

Calories per serving: 263; Carbohydrates: 22.3g; Protein: 5.6g; Fat: 18.5g; Sugar: 15.2g; Sodium: 65mg; Fiber: 5.3g

BERRY-CHOCO GOODNESS SHAKE

Serves: 1

Ingredients:

- ½ cup whole milk yogurt
- 1 packet Stevia, or more to taste
- ¼ cup raspberries
- ¼ cup Blackberry
- ¼ cup strawberries, chopped
- 1 tbsp cocoa powder
- 1 tbsp avocado oil
- 1 ½ cups water

Instructions:

1. Add all ingredients in blender.
2. Blend until smooth and creamy.
3. Serve and enjoy.

Nutrition information:

Calories per serving: 255; Carbohydrates: 20.2g; Protein: 6.4g; Fat: 19.2g; Sugar: 11.0g; Sodium: 66mg; Fiber: 6.3g

LEMONY-AVOCADO CILANTRO SHAKE

Serves: 1

Ingredients:
- ½ cup whole milk yogurt
- 1 packet Stevia, or more to taste
- 1 whole avocado
- 1 tbsp chopped cilantro
- 1 ½ cups water

Instructions:
1. Add all ingredients in blender.
2. Blend until smooth and creamy.
3. Serve and enjoy.

Nutrition information:
Calories per serving: 397; Carbohydrates: 23.4g; Protein: 8.3g; Fat: 33.4g; Sugar: 7.0g; Sodium: 78mg; Fiber: 13.5g

STRAWBERRY-CHOCOLATE YOGURT SHAKE

Serves: 1

Ingredients:

- ½ cup whole milk yogurt
- 1 packet Stevia, or more to taste
- ½ cup strawberries, chopped
- 1 tbsp cocoa powder
- 1 tbsp coconut oil
- 1 tbsp pepitas
- 1 ½ cups water

Instructions:

1. Add all ingredients in blender.
2. Blend until smooth and creamy.
3. Serve and enjoy.

Nutrition information:

Calories per serving: 269; Carbohydrates: 16.5g; Protein: g; Fat: 7.9g; Sugar: 9.4g; Sodium: 67mg; Fiber: 3.5g

Milk-Based Keto-Approved Smoothie & Shake Recipes

Choco-Coco Milk Shake

Serves: 1

Ingredients:
- ½ cup whole milk
- 1 tbsp cocoa powder
- 1 packet Stevia, or more to taste
- 1 tbsp coconut flakes, unsweetened
- 1 cup water
- 1 tbsp coconut oil

Instructions:
1. Add all ingredients in blender.
2. Blend until smooth and creamy.
3. Serve and enjoy.

Nutrition information:

Calories per serving: 263; Carbohydrates: 22.7g; Protein: 4.8g; Fat: 20.65g; Sugar: 14.7g; Sodium: 75mg; Fiber: 2.1g

NUTTY CHOCO MILK SHAKE

Serves: 1

Ingredients:

- ¼ cup whole milk
- 1 tbsp cocoa powder
- 1 packet Stevia, or more to taste
- ¼ cup pecans
- 1 ½ cups water
- 1 tbsp macadamia oil

Instructions:

1. Add all ingredients in blender.
2. Blend until smooth and creamy.
3. Serve and enjoy.

Nutrition information:

Calories per serving: 358; Carbohydrates: 15.5g; Protein: 5.1g; Fat: 34.0g; Sugar: 8.9g; Sodium: 33mg; Fiber: 4g

GRITTY CHOCO MILK SHAKE

Serves: 1

Ingredients:

- ¼ cup whole milk
- 1 tbsp cocoa powder
- 1 packet Stevia, or more to taste
- 1 tbsp chia seeds
- 1 tbsp hemp seeds
- 1 tbsp flaxseed
- 1 ½ cups water
- 1 tbsp Flaxseed oil

Instructions:

1. Add all ingredients in blender.
2. Blend until creamy yet still gritty. If preferred, blend until smooth.
3. Serve and enjoy.

Nutrition information:

Calories per serving: 363; Carbohydrates: 22.8g; Protein: 8.9g; Fat: 29.4g; Sugar: 8.3g; Sodium: 42mg; Fiber: 10.1g

CREAMY CHOCO SHAKE

Serves: 1

Ingredients:

- ½ cup heavy cream
- 2 tbsps cocoa powder
- 1 packet Stevia, or more to taste
- 1 cup water

Instructions:

1. Add all ingredients in blender.
2. Blend until smooth and creamy.
3. Serve and enjoy.

Nutrition information:

Calories per serving: 435; Carbohydrates: 10.6g; Protein: 4.6g; Fat: 45.5g; Sugar: 3.5g; Sodium: 52mg; Fiber: 4g

RASPBERRY-CHOCO SHAKE

Serves: 1

Ingredients:

- ½ cup heavy cream, liquid
- 1 tbsp cocoa powder
- 1 packet Stevia, or more to taste
- ¼ cup raspberries
- 1 ½ cups water

Instructions:

1. Add all ingredients in blender.
2. Blend until smooth and creamy.
3. Serve and enjoy.

Nutrition information:

Calories per serving: 438; Carbohydrates: 11.1g; Protein: 3.8g; Fat: 45.0g; Sugar: 4.8g; Sodium: 54mg; Fiber: 3.6g

STRAWBERRY-CHOCO SHAKE

Serves: 1

Ingredients:

- ½ cup heavy cream, liquid
- 1 tbsp cocoa powder
- 1 packet Stevia, or more to taste
- ½ cup strawberry, sliced
- 1 tbsp coconut flakes, unsweetened
- 1 ½ cups water

Instructions:

1. Add all ingredients in blender.
2. Blend until smooth and creamy.
3. Serve and enjoy.

Nutrition information:

Calories per serving: 470; Carbohydrates: 15.7g; Protein: 4.1g; Fat: 46.4g; Sugar: 8.9g; Sodium: 69mg; Fiber: 3.6g

ALMOND CHOCO SHAKE

Serves: 1

Ingredients:

- ½ cup heavy cream, liquid
- 1 tbsp cocoa powder
- 1 packet Stevia, or more to taste
- ½ cup almonds, chopped
- 1 ½ cups water

Instructions:

1. Soak almonds in water for at least 30 minutes.
2. Then, add all ingredients in blender.
3. Blend until smooth and creamy.
4. Serve and enjoy.

Nutrition information:

Calories per serving: 485; Carbohydrates: 15.7g; Protein: 11.9g; Fat: 45.9g; Sugar: 3.8g; Sodium: 31mg; Fiber: 7.4g

GRITTY AND NUTTY SHAKE

Serves: 1

Ingredients:

- ¼ cup heavy cream, liquid
- ½ tbsp cocoa powder
- 1 packet Stevia, or more to taste
- ¼ cup almonds, sliced
- ¼ cup macadamia nuts, whole
- 1 tbsp flaxseed
- 1 tbsp hemp seed
- 1 cup water

Instructions:

1. Add all ingredients in blender.
2. Blend until smooth and creamy.
3. Serve and enjoy.

Nutrition information:

Calories per serving: 590; Carbohydrates: 17.7g; Protein: 12.3g; Fat: 57.2g; Sugar: 3.8g; Sodium: 22mg; Fiber: 10.1g

NUTTY GREENS SHAKE

Serves: 1

Ingredients:

- ½ cup heavy cream, liquid
- 1 packet Stevia, or more to taste
- ¼ cup pecans
- ¼ macadamia nuts
- 1 ½ cups water
- 1 cup Spring mix salad greens

Instructions:

1. Add all ingredients in blender.
2. Blend until smooth and creamy.
3. Serve and enjoy.

Nutrition information:

Calories per serving: 628; Carbohydrates: 12.5g; Protein: 7.0g; Fat: 65.6g; Sugar: 4.7g; Sodium: 48mg; Fiber: 6.4g

RASPBERRY AND GREENS SHAKE

Serves: 1

Ingredients:
- 1 cup whole milk
- 1 packet Stevia, or more to taste
- ¼ cup Raspberry
- 1 cup water
- 1 tbsp macadamia oil
- 1 cup Spinach

Instructions:
1. Add all ingredients in blender.
2. Blend until smooth and creamy.
3. Serve and enjoy.

Nutrition information:

Calories per serving: 292; Carbohydrates: 17.43g; Protein: 8.9g; Fat: 21.9g; Sugar: 13.8g; Sodium: 136mg; Fiber: 2.7g

SPICED ALMOND SHAKE

Serves: 1

Ingredients:
- ½ cup whole milk
- 1 tbsp cocoa powder
- 1 packet Stevia, or more to taste
- ¼ cup almonds, sliced
- ½ tsp cinnamon
- ¼ tsp allspice
- ¼ tsp nutmeg
- 1 cup water
- 1 tbsp almond oil

Instructions:
1. Add all ingredients in blender.
2. Blend until smooth and creamy.
3. Serve and enjoy.

Nutrition information:

Calories per serving: 347; Carbohydrates: 16.6g; Protein: 9.8g; Fat: 30.1g; Sugar: 7.3g; Sodium: 59mg; Fiber: 5.4g

Cinnamon-Choco Coffee Milk Shake

Serves: 1

Ingredients:

- 1 cup whole milk
- 1 tbsp cocoa powder
- 1 cup brewed coffee, chilled
- ½ tsp cinnamon
- 1 packet Stevia, or more to taste
- 1 tbsp coconut oil

Instructions:

1. Add all ingredients in blender.
2. Blend until smooth and creamy.
3. Serve and enjoy.

Nutrition information:

Calories per serving: 284; Carbohydrates: 16.9g; Protein: 9g; Fat: 22.3g; Sugar: 12.4g; Sodium: 111mg; Fiber: 2.3g

MOCHA MILK SHAKE

Serves: 1

Ingredients:

- 1 cup whole milk
- 2 tbsps cocoa powder
- 2 packet Stevia, or more to taste
- 1 cup brewed coffee, chilled
- 1 tbsp coconut oil

Instructions:

1. Add all ingredients in blender.
2. Blend until smooth and creamy.
3. Serve and enjoy.

Nutrition information:

Calories per serving: 293; Carbohydrates: 19.9g; Protein: 10.1g; Fat: 23.1g; Sugar: 12.5g; Sodium: 112mg; Fiber: 4g

Coconut-Mocha Shake

Serves: 1

Ingredients:

- 3/4 cup whole milk
- 2 tbsps cocoa powder
- 1 tbsp coconut flakes, unsweetened
- 2 packet Stevia, or more to taste
- 1 cup brewed coffee, chilled
- 1 tbsp coconut oil

Instructions:

1. Add all ingredients in blender.
2. Blend until smooth and creamy.
3. Serve and enjoy.

Nutrition information:

Calories per serving: 280; Carbohydrates: 19.75g; Protein: 8.33g; Fat: 22.6g; Sugar: 11.4g; Sodium: 101mg; Fiber: 4.5g

NUTRITIOUSLY GREEN MILK SHAKE

Serves: 1

Ingredients:

- 1 cup whole milk
- 1 packet Stevia, or more to taste
- 1 tbsp coconut flakes, unsweetened
- 1 cup water
- 2 cups Spring Mix Salad
- 1 tbsp coconut oil

Instructions:

1. Add all ingredients in blender.
2. Blend until smooth and creamy.
3. Serve and enjoy.

Nutrition information:

Calories per serving: 309; Carbohydrates: 18.9g; Protein: 9.5g; Fat: 23.3g; Sugar: 15.3g; Sodium: 157mg; Fiber: 2.7g

Made in the USA
Monee, IL
10 September 2019